CAMBRIDGE
UNIVERSITY PRESS

CAMBRIDGE ENGLISH
Language Assessment
Part of the University of Cambridge

CAMBRIDGE
OFFICIAL
PREPARATION MATERIAL

Updated
Second Edition

T0372769

Workbook 4
with Online Resources
American English

Caroline Nixon & Michael Tomlinson

Cambridge University Press
www.cambridge.org/elt

Cambridge Assessment English
www.cambridgeenglish.org

Information on this title: www.cambridge.org/9781316627204

© Cambridge University Press 2008, 2015, 2017

First published 2008
Second edition 2015
Updated second edition 2017

20 19 18 17 16

Printed in Great Britain by Ashford Colour Press Ltd.

A catalog record for this publication is available from the British Library

ISBN 978-1-316-62720-4 Workbook with Online Resources 4
ISBN 978-1-316-62754-9 Student's Book 4
ISBN 978-1-316-62703-7 Teacher's Book 4
ISBN 978-1-316-62726-6 Class Audio CDs 4
ISBN 978-1-316-62737-2 Teacher's Resource Book with Online Audio 4
ISBN 978-1-316-63013-6 Flashcards 4 (pack of 103)
ISBN 978-1-316-62790-7 Interactive DVD with Teacher's Booklet 4 (PAL/NTSC)
ISBN 978-1-316-62711-2 Presentation Plus 4
ISBN 978-1-316-63018-1 Posters 4

Additional resources for this publication at www.cambridge.org/elt/kidsboxamericanenglish

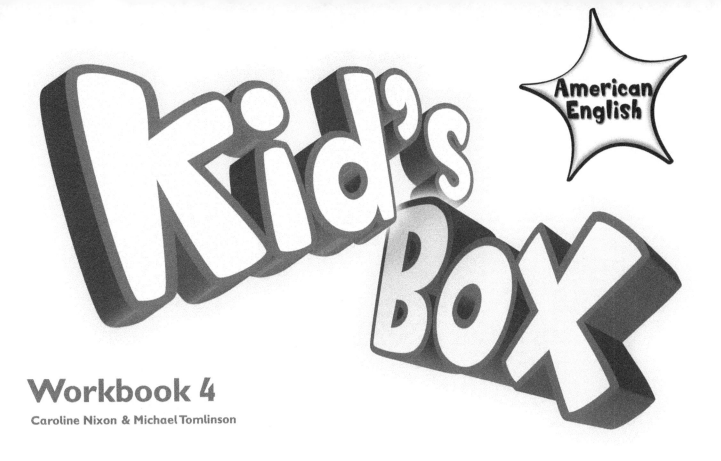

American English

Kid's Box

Workbook 4

Caroline Nixon & Michael Tomlinson

Hello there!

1 Read and circle.

1 Their dog's **dirtier** / **cleaner** than their cat.
2 Grandpa Star's **younger** / **older** than Mr. Star.
3 Sally's **taller** / **shorter** than Suzy.
4 Aunt May's hair is **shorter** / **longer** than Uncle Fred's hair.
5 Mr. Star's **smaller** / **bigger** than Scott.
6 Grandma Star's **happier** / **sadder** than Mrs. Star.

2 Complete the sentences.

1 Lily wants to play _badminton_ .
2 Jim wants to go _____ .
3 Vicky and Danny want to _____ .
4 Stacey wants to _____ .
5 Daisy wants _____ .
6 Fred and Paul _____ .
7 Charlie _____ .

① ② ③ ④ ⑤ ⑥ ⑦

3 Unscramble and write the words.

olcd

_____

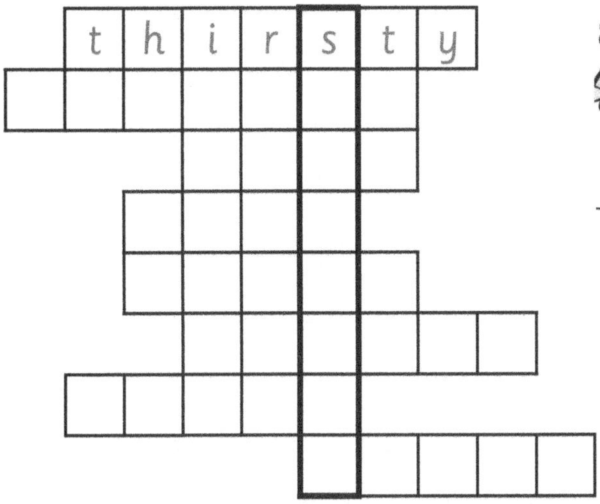

nhguyr

_____

sthrtiy
thirsty

tsamr

_____

augnhty

_____

dlou

_____

uqiet

_____

itrde

_____

Crossword grid (across top): t h i r s t y

4 Kid's Box File.

My name's _____.

I'm _____ years old. I have _____ _____ hair and _____ eyes.

There are _____ people in my family.

Their names are _____

_____.

I like _____ and _____.

I don't like _____.

My favorite _____ is _____.

5 Ask your friend. Complete the questionnaire.

	always	sometimes	never
1 Do you wake up at six o'clock?	☐	☐	☐
2 Do you have breakfast in the kitchen?	☐	☐	☐
3 Do you have lunch at school?	☐	☐	☐
4 Do you watch TV after school?	☐	☐	☐
5 Do you go to bed at nine o'clock?	☐	☐	☐
6 Do you go to the park on weekends?	☐	☐	☐

6 Write about your friend.

1 _My friend Danny always wakes up at six o'clock._
2 _My friend_ _____ _has breakfast_ _____
3 _My_ _____ _has_ _____
4 _My_ _____ _watches_ _____
5 _____ _goes_ _____
6 _____

7 Read and match.

1 Hello, Jack. How are you?
 `c`

2 How old are you?
 ☐

3 What's your name?
 ☐

4 Who's that?
 ☐

5 Whose bike is this?
 ☐

6 Whose tractor is that?
 ☐

a It's my aunt's.
b That's my uncle, Paul.
c I'm fine, thanks.
d It's my uncle's.
e I'm ten.
f Mary.

8 Look. Write "before" or "after." Match.

1 She gets up __after__ she wakes up. [b]

2 She washes _____ she has breakfast. ☐

3 She gets dressed _____ she washes. ☐

4 She has breakfast _____ she brushes her teeth. ☐

5 She combs her hair _____ she gets her bag. ☐

6 She catches the bus _____ she puts on her shoes. ☐

9 Circle the one that doesn't belong.

1 (pants)	teacher	doctor	dentist	farmer
2 floor	door	window	stairs	bus
3 library	hospital	supermarket	movies	truck
4 bear	snake	rock	lion	bat
5 river	lake	ocean	blanket	waterfall
6 plant	grass	cook	tree	leaf
7 son	aunt	driver	uncle	daughter
8 sunny	hot	island	windy	cloudy
9 coat	scarf	hat	sweater	dentist
10 longer	quieter	teacher	shorter	bigger

10 **07** **Write. Listen, check, and say.**

CD1

> ~~name~~ bag start play stand farmer straight
> man far have gray car catch take artist

s**a**d	r**ai**n	c**ar**
	name	

11 **Change one letter to make new words.**

1 A color.
2 You sleep in this.
3 Not good.
4 This animal sleeps during the day.
5 This animal likes eating fish.
6 We can drive this.
7 We listen with this.
8 When you're hungry, you ... .
9 You wear this on your head.

red
hat

 Ha! Ha! Ha!

What do you call a fish with no eyes?

JOKE BOX

fish.

12 **Write the numbers and connect the dots.**

Start at number **68**. Find another picture with the same thing in it. Look, there's a plant in **68**, and there's a plant in **39**. Write number **39** in the box.

68	39										

Now connect the dots.

What is the picture? _____

1 Back to school

1 Find the words.

busy   exciting   boring   careful   difficult   ~~brave~~   slow   quick   terrible

d	z	e	x	s	b	r	a	v	e	a
i	p	h	c	u	f	b	m	e	v	r
f	w	w	a	r	j	i	m	x	c	e
f	z	a	r	p	j	n	f	c	r	k
i	n	l	e	r	e	s	p	i	n	p
c	q	h	f	i	k	l	q	t	p	e
u	u	b	u	s	y	o	h	i	g	u
l	i	j	l	e	i	w	l	n	f	h
t	c	g	b	o	r	i	n	g	d	k
u	k	r	t	e	r	r	i	b	l	e

2 Look at the pictures. Complete the sentences.

1 The man's getting the boy. He's very **b** _rave_ .

2 My aunt thinks television is **b**_____ .

3 My younger sister thinks it's **d**_____ to put her shoes on.

4 You must be **c**_____ when you cross the street.

5 We were at the beach yesterday. It was windy and cold.
The weather was **t**_____ .

6 The snail is a small animal. It's very **s**_____ .

7 What a great motorcycle. It's really **q**_____!

8 This book is very **e**_____ . I don't want to go to bed.

9 My mom is **b**_____ because she works a lot.

3 Complete the questionnaire.

Me

1 I think music lessons are   boring ☐   easy ☐   exciting ☐

2 I think television is   exciting ☐   terrible ☐   boring ☐

3 I think math classes are   easy ☐   difficult ☐   exciting ☐

4 I think soccer is   exciting ☐   boring ☐   terrible ☐

5 I think computer games are   terrible ☐   exciting ☐   difficult ☐

6 When I do my homework, I am   careful ☐   quick ☐   slow ☐

7 When I go to school, I am   quick ☐   slow ☐   careful ☐

4 Ask your friend. Write the answers.

What do you think of computer games?

I think they're exciting.

1 What do you think of computer games? _exciting_ _____

2 What do you think of television? _____

3 What do you think of tennis? _____

4 What do you think of school? _____

5 What do you think of pop music? _____

6 What do you think of comic books? _____

7 What do you think of soccer? _____

5 🔊 **CD1 12** Listen and draw lines. Color.

| Paul | Jane | Mr. Edison | Danny | Mary | Jim |

6 Read and circle the correct answer.

1 This is the person | when / (who) / when | teaches children.

2 There | are / is / have | five children in the classroom.

3 Mr. Edison's the teacher | what / when / who | is writing on the board.

4 Mary's the girl | where / with / who | is wearing a pink dress.

5 Paul's book is | in / under / on | the desk.

6 Jim's the boy | who / with / why | is sharpening his pencil.

7 Danny's talking | about / to / for | Mary.

8 In the classroom the children | must / can't / must not | listen to the teacher.

7 Look at the pictures. Read and correct.

black beard

1 The man who's painting has a ~~gray mustache.~~

2 The man who's throwing a ball has a little white dog.

3 The woman who teaches music lives in a tall building.

4 The man who has a mustache rides his horse to school.

5 The woman who likes books gets up at nine o'clock.

8 Read and complete the chart.

There are four new teachers at KB Elementary School.

Name	Description	Age	Subject	Hobby
		42	English	
Miss Stone				
		28		playing the guitar
	curly gray hair		Music	

1 The woman who teaches music likes reading. She's 57.
2 The teacher who's 42 has a black beard. His name's Mr. Brown.
3 The woman who's 30 has long fair hair. She teaches math.
4 The man who likes playing the guitar has a brown mustache.
5 The man who likes playing tennis teaches English.
6 The woman who teaches math likes horseback riding.
7 The man who doesn't teach English teaches P.E. His name's Mr. Kelly.
8 The woman who's 57 is Mrs. Bird.

9 16 **Write. Listen, check, and say.**
CD1

s<u>i</u>t	s<u>ee</u>	f<u>i</u>v<u>e</u>
quick	----------	----------
----------	----------	----------
----------	----------	----------
----------	----------	----------
----------	----------	----------

easy	smile
~~quick~~	time
night	busy
fly	teach
give	me
think	buy
key	need
finish	

10 **Read and write the words.**

1 She's Sally's friend, but she's older than Sally is. _Eva_
2 A person who works in a hospital. ----------
3 The opposite of "always." ----------
4 A person who looks at teeth every day. ----------
5 There are a lot of these in a forest. Monkeys
   sometimes live in them. ----------
6 The opposite of "difficult." ----------
7 This little animal is very slow. ----------

11 **Cross out the words from Activity 10.**

new	~~Eva~~	dentist	likes	doctor	teacher
never	Robert	snail	trees	his	easy

Use the other words to write a sentence.

---------- ---------- ---------- ---------- ----------

Ha! Ha! Ha!

Why is the math book sad?

Because it has a lot of problems.

JOKE BOX

Do you remember?

 Look and read
 Say
 Fold the page
 Write the words
 Correct

 _huge_ --------------

 ----

 --------------

 --------------

 --------------

 ----

 --------------

 --------------

 --------------

 huge

 exciting

 brave

 careful

 difficult

 little

 slow

 quick

 terrible

Can do

I can describe people.

I can describe things.

I can say what I think.

15

1 Look and write the number.

1 13.91 m   Thirteen meters ninety-one centimeters.

2 20.47 m   _____

3 35.69 m   _____

4 41.54 m   _____

5 78.10 m   _____

6 92.15 m   _____

7 83.12 m   _____

8 64.27 m   _____

2 Read and answer.

1 Danny is 1.25 m tall. His friend Sam is 19 cm taller than he is. How tall is Sam?
   He's one meter forty-four centimeters.

2 Vicky's mom is 9 cm shorter than her dad. Her dad's height is 1.83 m. How tall is Vicky's mom?

   _____

3 The new baby elephant at Park Zoo is 79 cm tall. Its mother is 3.17 m taller than the baby. How tall is the mother?

   _____

4 Fred's backyard is 1.62 m longer than Grace's backyard. Her backyard is 14.11 m long. How long is Fred's backyard?

   _____

5 Daisy's school is 5.78 m high. Jack's school is 1.13 m higher than Daisy's. How high is Jack's school?

   _____

3 Read the story. Choose a word from the box. Write the correct word next to numbers 1–5. There is one example.

My name is Stacey. My dad's a _farmer_____, and I live on a big farm in the country. We have about eighty (1) _____ and thirty cows. My dad's always busy, and he sometimes works at (2) _____! On Saturdays and Sundays, I sometimes help my dad with the animals.

I don't want to be a farmer, I want to be an art (3) _____. I study art in school, but I have only two lessons a week, and I want to (4) _____ better pictures.

Every Friday afternoon, after school, my aunt and I catch the bus to the city center. My aunt goes shopping, and I have an art lesson, a longer one. It's never (5) _____, it's exciting!

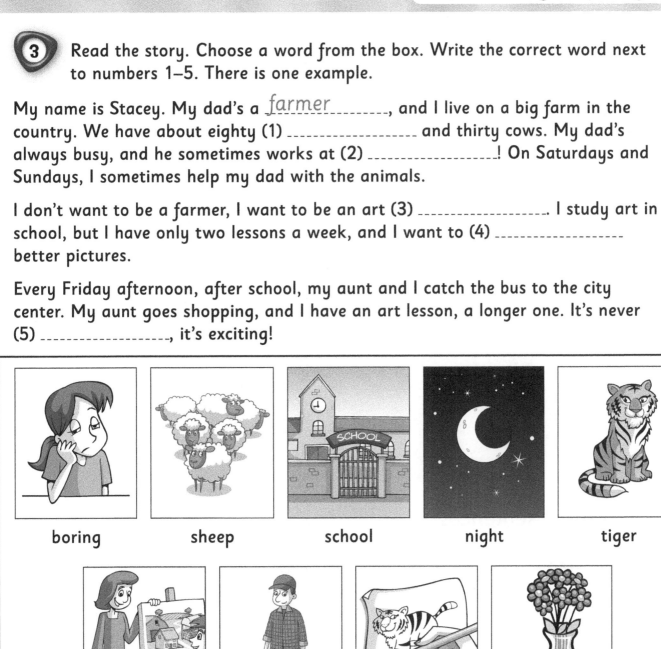

boring   sheep   school   night   tiger

teacher   farmer   draw   pretty

(6) Now choose the best name for the story.
    Check one box.

    Stacey wants to be a farmer   ☐

    Stacey goes shopping with her aunt   ☐

    Stacey wants to be an art teacher   ☐

2 Good sports

1 🔊 **21** **CD1** Listen and draw lines.

Jane

Jim

Mary

Fred

Jack

Daisy

Danny

2 Write the sentences.

| tennis | I | difficult. | think | is |

1 I _____ think _____ tennis _____ is _____ difficult. _____

| learn | sail. | to | can | We |

2 _____ _____ _____ _____ _____

| She's | who | skating. | the girl | likes |

3 _____ _____ _____ _____ _____

| play | can | You | inside. | basketball |

4 _____ _____ _____ _____ _____

| you | fishing? | want | Do | to go |

5 _____ _____ _____ _____ _____

3 Read and complete the chart.

Paul, Jim, Sue, and Mary are at the Sports Center. They want to do different things.

Name	Age	Sport	Equipment
			a big ball
		swim	
Sue			
	12		

1 The boy who's twelve wants to climb. He needs strong shoes and a helmet.
2 Mary wants to swim, so she needs a towel.
3 Mary and Paul are both twelve.
4 Jim is eleven, and Sue is ten.
5 The girl who's ten wants to roller-skate. She needs some roller skates and a helmet.
6 The boy who's eleven wants to play volleyball. He needs a big ball.

4 Write the words.

1 What do we call people who teach?   teachers
2 What do we call people who dance?   ------------------
3 What do we call people who climb?   ------------------
4 What do we call people who swim?   ------------------
5 What do we call people who ice-skate?   ------------------
6 What do we call people who win?   ------------------
7 What do we call people who sing?   ------------------

5 Read and circle the correct answer. Match.

1 She's writing **careful** / **carefully**.
2 They're running **quickly** / **quick**.
3 We're drawing **bad** / **badly**.
4 I'm walking **slow** / **slowly**.
5 He's reading **well** / **good**.
6 You're speaking **quietly** / **quiet**.

6 Complete the sentences about you. Use the words in the box.

badly   well   slowly   quickly   carefully   loudly   quietly

1 I sing   _badly_.
2 I play tennis   _____.
3 I write   _____.
4 I read   _____.
5 I ride my bike   _____.
6 I eat   _____.
7 I drink   _____.
8 I sometimes walk _____.
9 I play the guitar _____.
10 I sometimes talk _____.

7 Now ask a friend.

Do you sing badly?

No, I sing really well.

Do you … ?

No, … .

8 Read. Unscramble and write the words.

1 A place where you can practice soccer inside.
   (ecstrponerts)   _sports center_
2 A place where you can fish. (ervri)   _____
3 A place where you can go roller-skating. (akpr) _____
4 A place where you can sail. (aelk)   _____
5 A place where you can climb trees. (efrsto)   _____
6 A place where you can swim in the ocean. (abceh) _____

9 Read and match.

1. We're shouting loudly
2. She's talking quietly
3. He's walking slowly
4. You're running quickly
5. They're winning
6. She's carrying the boxes carefully
7. I need an eraser

a. because your school bus is going.
b. because she doesn't want to drop them.
c. because I'm drawing very badly.
d. because he has a backache.
e. because she's in the library.
f. because they're playing well.
g. because we're watching an exciting soccer game.

10 Read and complete the chart.

	swim	play soccer	play the piano	sing	write	climb	draw
Alex							
Eva							
Robert		well	badly				
Suzy							
Scott							
Sally							

1 The person who plays soccer well plays the piano badly.
2 The person who swims quickly sings quietly.
3 The person who writes well swims slowly.
4 The person who sings loudly writes slowly.
5 The person who plays the piano well climbs carefully.
6 The person who climbs quickly draws well.

11 **27** Write. Listen, check, and say.

CD1

1 We can see __whales__ in the ocean.
2 In _____ we learn about the heart.
3 Vicky's _____ a story about a detective.
4 I always _____ to school.
5 What's the _____ to that question?
6 I want to go to an _____ for my next vacation.
7 The teacher says we _____ talk in the library.
8 I love _____ mountains.
9 John likes _____ to pop music.
10 What's her name? I don't _____ .

island
~~whales~~
know
science
climbing
walk
shouldn't
listening
writing
answer

12 Complete the crossword puzzle.

What's this sport? _____

	1	o	u	t	s	i	d	e	

1 The opposite of inside.
2 Hair on a man's face. It's under his mouth.
3 Grandpa Star loves going to the river to catch fish. He loves _____.
4 We can play games, run, and jump here.
5 The opposite of easy.
6 A person who paints pictures.

Ha! Ha! Ha!

Why can't you play baseball in the afternoon?

Because the bats like to sleep in the day.

JOKE BOX

Do you remember?

 Look and read
 Say
 Fold the page
 Write the words
 Correct

 *inside* _____

 _____

 _____

 _____

 _____

 _____

 _____

 _____

 _____

 _____

 inside

 outside

 fish

 dance

 sail

 skate

 climb

 run

 skip rope

 swim

Can do

I can say more action verbs.

I can talk about how I do things.

I can say what I want to do.

1 Order the sentences.

batter

In baseball the person who hits the ball is called the batter. The person who throws the ball to the batter is called the pitcher.

The winning team is the team with more runs at the end of the game. ☐

In baseball there are two teams with nine players each. This is how you play: 1

Next the batter hits the ball. He or she has to run very quickly. ☐

He or she runs to first base. ☐

First the pitcher throws the ball. ☐

After that he or she runs to third base. ☐

Then he or she runs to second base. ☐

When the batter gets to home plate, he or she gets a "run." ☐

pitcher

2 Write about soccer. Use these words.

soccer / two teams / eleven players each
first / player from one team / kick ball
players / run / kick / ball
both teams / try / score goals
winning team / more goals / ninety minutes

In soccer there are

Listen and color and write. There is one example.

Review Units  1 and 2

(1) Answer the questions.

1 What's the second letter in 🖼 ?   ..a..

2 What's the third letter in 🛼 ?   ------

3 What's the first letter in 🎹 ?   ------

4 What's the first letter in 🪖 ?   ------

5 What's the third letter in 🐌 ?   ------

6 What's the first letter in 🏸 ?   ------

7 What's the fifth letter in ⚽ ?   ------

8 What's the first letter in 🎾 ?   ------

What's the word? _____

(2) What's wrong with these pictures? Write the answers.

1 The bat has a
   long beard.
   _____

2 _____
   _____

3 _____
   _____
   _____

4 _____
   _____

5 _____
   _____

6 _____
   _____

3 Circle the one that doesn't belong.

1 (eight)	first	second	third
2 run	quick	jump	roller-skate
3 well	badly	slowly	tall
4 busy	careful	vacation	terrible
5 earache	music	P.E.	math
6 class	teacher	weather	school
7 thirty	first	ninety	forty
8 running	jumping	shopping	swimming
9 family	aunt	uncle	beard
10 skate	famous	difficult	exciting
11 hair	mustache	beard	climb
12 bike	run	swim	hop

4 Now complete the crossword puzzle. Write the message.

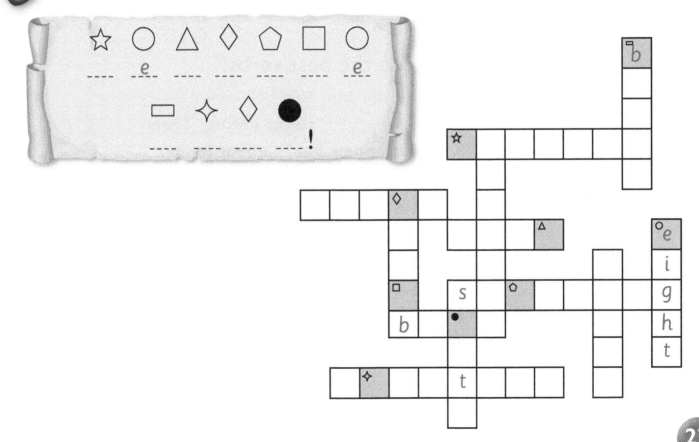

27

3 Health matters

1 Read Sally's diary.

> **Friday**
>
> I had a busy day. In the morning I ate a big breakfast and drank a lot of milk. I went to school with Suzy. Before lunch I had my favorite classes, math and science. I saw my music teacher and took her my project. It's my new song. After lunch, our English teacher gave us a test. There were 20 questions. I was the first to finish!

Now look for the past of the verbs.

1 is   _was_   **6** see   _____
2 have _____   **7** take _____
3 eat _____   **8** give _____
4 drink _____   **9** are _____
5 go _____

2 Complete the diary. Use the past verbs.

> After school I (1) _went_ _____ to the library. There
> (2) _____ a lot of new books about famous
> people. I (3) _____ my science teacher at the
> library. She (4) _____ me a book on Marie Curie,
> and I (5) _____ another book on detectives for
> Scott. He (6) _____ at home in bed because he
> (7) _____ a cold. We (8) _____
> hamburgers and fries for dinner, and I (9) _____
> some more milk before I went to bed. I love milk!

3 Choose the words.

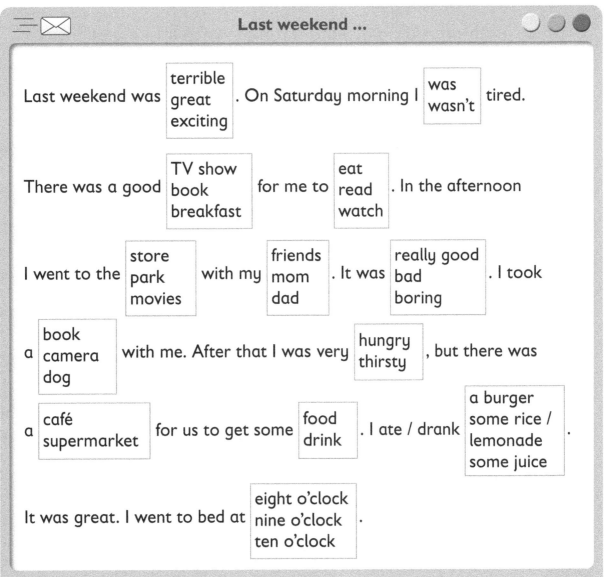

Last weekend ...

Last weekend was [terrible / great / exciting]. On Saturday morning I [was / wasn't] tired.

There was a good [TV show / book / breakfast] for me to [eat / read / watch]. In the afternoon

I went to the [store / park / movies] with my [friends / mom / dad]. It was [really good / bad / boring]. I took

a [book / camera / dog] with me. After that I was very [hungry / thirsty], but there was

a [café / supermarket] for us to get some [food / drink]. I ate / drank [a burger / some rice / lemonade / some juice].

It was great. I went to bed at [eight o'clock / nine o'clock / ten o'clock].

4 Now write about your weekend.

Last weekend was _____

_____

_____

_____

_____

_____

_____

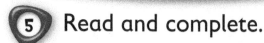

5 **Read and complete.**

Five children are sitting around a table. We're looking at them from above.

1 The girl sitting between Paul and Jack gave her mom some flowers yesterday. She didn't have lunch at school. Her name is Susan.
2 Paul didn't see his friends in the afternoon. He did his homework.
3 Daisy went to a party in the afternoon.

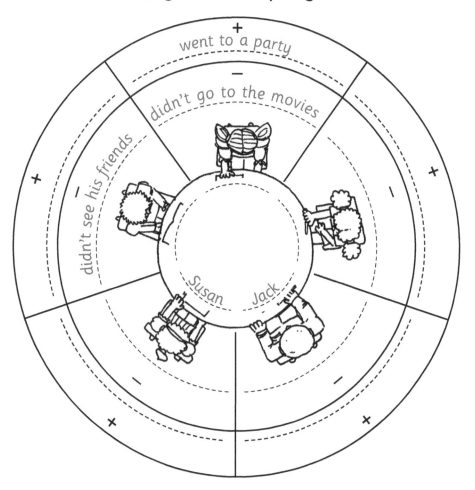

4 The girl who didn't go to a party or give her mom flowers saw a movie at the movie theater in the afternoon. Her name is Stacey.
5 The boy who's sitting next to Stacey had a stomachache, so he didn't eat any food all day.
6 The girl who didn't go to the movies yesterday is sitting between Paul and Stacey.
7 Stacey didn't drink any milk at breakfast.

6 **Write sentences about the children.**

1 _Paul did his homework. He didn't see his friends in the afternoon._
2 _____
3 _____
4 _____
5 _____

7 Put the words in groups.

> chicken cousin burger teacher mom
> milk school lemonade hospital banana
> movie theater juice park water nurse apple

Places: _____

People: _____

Food: _chicken_____

Drink: _____

8 Use the words from Activity 7 to complete Eva's day.

	go	see	eat	drink
morning	hospital			
afternoon		cousin		
evening				

9 Ask and answer. Complete the chart.

Did Eva go to the hospital in the morning? Yes, she did.

Did she see the nurse? No, she didn't.

	go	see	eat	drink
morning				
afternoon				
evening				

10 🔊 37 CD1 **Write. Listen, check, and say.**

1 Let's go _fishing_ . It's a lot of fun!
2 Fred's very fast. He's a good _____ player, too.
3 You must eat a lot of fruit and _____ .
4 _____ plays volleyball with her best friend.
5 Ben's a big _____ . He's very tall, too!
6 Basketball's a _____ fast game.
7 Vera visits her grandmother's _____ on Fridays.
8 Bill took a _____ of his father playing baseball.
9 Look at the baby with the big blue _____ !
10 Oh! Look at those _____ flowers!

> village
> ~~fishing~~
> volleyball
> balloon
> vegetables
> boy
> very
> Vicky
> beautiful
> photograph

 11 **Make sentences.**

~~Mary~~	the	to the	the hospital.
Jim didn't	~~had~~	people at	~~cough.~~
Zoe saw	lot of	~~a terrible~~	her medicine?
Did	go	take	doctor.
There were a	Stacey	dentist	last week.

1 _Mary had a terrible cough._
2 _____
3 _____
4 _____
5 _____

 Ha! Ha! Ha!

Doctor, Doctor, I think I'm a sheep!

 JOKE BOX

That's baaaad.

Do you remember?

 Look and read   Say   Fold the page    Write the words   Correct

is	_was_		is	→	was
are			are	→	were
have			have	→	had
go			go	→	went
see			see	→	saw
eat			eat	→	ate
drink			drink	→	drank
give			give	→	gave
take			take	→	took
today	_yesterday_		today		yesterday
this afternoon			this afternoon		yesterday afternoon
tonight			tonight		last night
this week			this week		last week
this year			this year		last year

Can do

I can talk about health matters.

I can talk about the past.

I can ask questions in the past.

1 41 CD1 Listen and check. Read and correct.

a  ☐   b 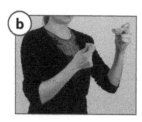 ✓   c 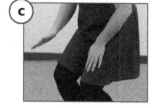 ☐

1 She's tapping her face.   No, she isn't. She's snapping her fingers.

a  ☐   b  ☐   c  ☐

2 He's using his mouth. _____

a  ☐   b  ☐   c  ☐

3 She's stamping her feet. _____

a 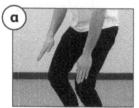 ☐   b 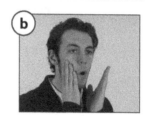 ☐   c  ☐

4 He's hitting his knees. _____

2 Read and complete.

| ~~body~~ percussion singing feet clap music different instrument |

The human (1) _body_ is a great musical (2) _____ and not
only for (3) _____ . We can make a lot of (4) _____ sounds.
When we (5) _____ our hands, snap our fingers, or stamp our
(6) _____ with rhythm, we are making (7) _____ . This kind
of music is called body (8) _____ .

Listen and write. There is one example.

At the doctor's

When? _yesterday_

1   What was the matter? _ache_

2   Can't eat:

3   Where was her aunt on Friday?

4   Her temperature:

5   She has to:

1 Complete the text. Use the past of the verbs.

Kim and Stacey had a great weekend. They went to an activity center in the country with their friend Paul.

On Saturday morning they
(1) _____started_____ (start) early. First they
(2) _____ (sail) on the lake. Then, in the afternoon they **(3)** _____ (climb) a mountain. In the evening they **(4)** _____ (cook) burgers outside. The children **(5)** _____ (talk) and **(6)** _____ (laugh) all evening.

On Sunday morning they **(7)** _____ (walk) in the forest. Their teacher **(8)** _____ (plant) a tree, and Kim, Stacey, and Paul **(9)** _____ (help) him.

In the afternoon they **(10)** _____ (play) games. They
(11) _____ (want) to stop at four o'clock because they
(12) _____ (need) to go home and sleep!

2 Read and write "yes" or "no."

1 Kim and Stacey had a boring weekend.	_____no_____
2 On Saturday morning they sailed on the lake.	_____
3 In the evening they cooked burgers inside.	_____
4 On Sunday afternoon they walked in the forest.	_____
5 Their teacher planted a tree.	_____
6 In the afternoon they played the piano.	_____
7 They stopped at five o'clock.	_____

3 Put the words in groups.

| like try stop sail play jump drop invite roller-skate |
| close shop cry skip shout dance climb carry hop |

+ed	+d	+ped	y+ied
sailed	liked	stopped	tried

4 Write the secret message.

¹ was	² at	³ supermarket	⁴ he	⁵ I	⁶ shouted
⁷ He	⁸ motorcycle	⁹ and	¹⁰ laughed	¹¹ Motors	¹² outside
¹³ him	¹⁴ tried	¹⁵ but	¹⁶ jumped	¹⁷ the	¹⁸ Nick
¹⁹ and	²⁰ our	²¹ to	²² pointed	²³ on	²⁴ catch

Lock,
5-14-21-24-18-11. 7-1-12-17-3. 5-22-2-13-9-6-,
15-4-10-9-16-23-20-8!

I tried

Key

5 Match and write.

fifth 5th

.... 3rd

.... 2nd

.... 9th

.... 1st

.... 12th

.... 20th

.... 8th

first   second   third

eighth   fifth   ninth

twentieth   twelfth

6 Find the letter. Write three words starting with that letter.

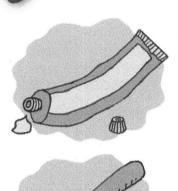

1 The ninth letter of "toothpaste."
tired, temperature, Thursday

2 The eighth letter of "baseball."
----

3 The fourth letter of "naughty."
----

4 The tenth letter of "downstairs."
----

5 The sixth letter of "outside."
----

6 The second letter of "yesterday."
----

7 The fifth letter of "strong."
----

8 The third letter of "kick."

Outside

Yesterday

Downstairs

7 **Read and answer.**

It's the first in "snail," but not in "mouse." `s`

It's the second in "school," but not in "house." ☐

It's the third in "apartment" and also in "stair." ☐

It's the fourth in "beard" and also in "hair." ☐

It's the fifth in "careful." Is it Lock's? ☐

Find the word. It's in Kid's Box! ----------------------

It's the first in "dog," but not in "cat." ☐

It's the second in "dress," but not in "hat." ☐

It's the third in "green" and also in "Fred." ☐

It's the fourth in "sweater" and also in "bread." ☐

It's the fifth in "swimming pool." Yes, that's right! ☐

We do this when we sleep at night. ----------------------

8 **Read and complete the chart.**

Name	Position	Activity
Daisy		
	Second	
		ice-skated

1 Jim, Daisy, Vicky, and Fred were in different competitions last weekend.
2 One danced, one ice-skated, one jumped, and one played Ping-Pong.
3 Vicky was fourth in her competition, and Jim was the boy who came third.
4 Daisy jumped in her competition.
5 Fred was the boy who danced.
6 The girl who came first didn't play Ping-Pong.

9 **09** **CD2** Write. Listen, check, and say.

~~called~~ started sailed stopped kicked invited
rained wanted helped danced snowed decided

"d" – played	"t" – walked	"id" – needed
called		

10 Choose the right answers and complete the text.

1 call   (called)   calls   **5** climb   climbed   climed
2 us   we   our   **6** fifteenth   fifteen   fiveteenth
3 afternoon   two o'clock   Saturday   **7** called   cleaned   cooked
4 talk   play   listen   **8** waved   watched   washed

To: fred@kidsbox.com   From: scott@kidsbox.com

On Wednesday Alex (1) _called_ me. He invited (2) _____
to go to his house on (3) _____ to (4) _____ about the
school play.

We walked to Alex's house with Eva and Robert. We (5) _____
up to the (6) _____ floor. His mom (7) _____ fish for
lunch. Then we (8) _____ a movie on television. It was very funny.

Ha! Ha! Ha!

Why are you sad?
My teacher was angry with me for
something I didn't do. What was that?

My homework.

JOKE BOX

Do you remember?

 Look and read

 Say

 Fold the page

 Write the words

 Correct

1st	first	1st	first
2nd	_____	2nd	second
3rd	_____	3rd	third
4th	_____	4th	fourth
5th	_____	5th	fifth
6th	_____	6th	sixth
7th	_____	7th	seventh
8th	_____	8th	eighth
9th	_____	9th	ninth
10th	_____	10th	tenth
11th	_____	11th	eleventh
12th	_____	12th	twelfth
13th	_____	13th	thirteenth
14th	_____	14th	fourteenth
15th	_____	15th	fifteenth
16th	_____	16th	sixteenth
17th	_____	17th	seventeenth
18th	_____	18th	eighteenth
19th	_____	19th	nineteenth
20th	_____	20th	twentieth

Can do

I can say the numbers 1st through 20th.

I can talk about things I did yesterday.

I can ask questions about last week.

1 Read and think. Write "play," "poem," or "novel."

1 Actors say the words.	_play_
2 This can take you two or three weeks to read.	
3 This sometimes has words that rhyme.	
4 This is a long story in a book.	
5 We see this at the theater.	

2 Choose your poem.

The | bat / snail / frog | and the | giraffe / chicken / lizard | went to the | town / stars / beach

In a beautiful | sea-blue hat / leaf-green bed / snow-white box .

They took some | jeans / parrots / cheese | , and plenty of | carrots / peas / beans ,

Covered in | big clean socks / a purple rug / pieces of bread .

Listen and check (✓) the box. There is one example.

What did Daisy do on Saturday?

A ☐ B ✓ C ☐

3 What did Daisy and her friends do first?

A ☐ B ☐ C ☐

1 Who did Daisy go to the park with?

A ☐ B ☐ C ☐

4 What did they have for lunch?

A ☐ B ☐ C ☐

2 What time did they go to the park?

A ☐ B ☐ C ☐

5 How did Daisy and her friends go home?

A ☐ B ☐ C ☐

Review Units 3 and 4

1 Find the past of the verbs.

s	k	a	t	e	d	w	s	f	l	m
w	w	t	s	g	d	a	y	i	i	h
e	t	w	b	a	d	s	h	s	k	a
n	s	o	r	v	w	a	s	h	e	d
t	h	c	o	e	t	r	i	e	d	n
d	r	a	n	k	g	e	o	d	o	a
e	o	w	e	r	e	p	t	a	t	e

~~are~~   have   go   take   see
eat   drink   give   wash
try   is   like   fish   skate

2 Complete the sentences with words from Activity 1.

1 Jim __went__ to the hospital to see his grandmother.
2 Sue _____ a lot of water because she was thirsty.
3 Danny _____ sick last week, so he _____ the doctor.
4 Vicky _____ a bad cold, so she _____ some medicine last night.
5 Mary and Stacey _____ sick yesterday because they _____ a lot of chocolate.
6 Fred _____ his mother some flowers for her birthday.

3 Read and answer. Write "Yes, I did" or "No, I didn't."

1 Did you go to the movies last Saturday? _____
2 Did you get up early yesterday? _____
3 Did you play basketball last week? _____
4 Did you need a scarf yesterday? _____
5 Did you dance last weekend? _____

4 Circle the one that doesn't belong.

1	headache	mustache	earache	backache
2	between	behind	awake	down
3	quickly	worse	slowly	carefully
4	neck	back	shoulders	kick
5	library	hospital	writer	store
6	hurt	first	second	eighth
7	cry	carry	sailed	try
8	skip	danced	clap	hop
9	thirty	forty	sixty	twentieth
10	goes	shows	knows	cows
11	had	fun	went	gave
12	tired	pointed	started	shouted

5 Now complete the crossword puzzle. Write the message.

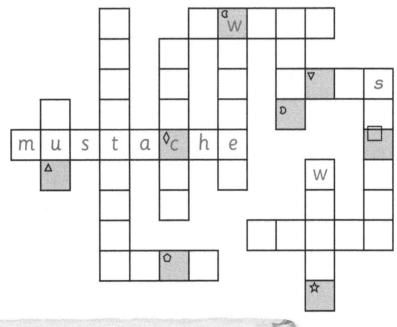

45

5 Exploring our world

1 Make sentences.

1 The explorer found
2 He caught a lot
3 They came
4 She took some
5 We made a
6 They got up
7 I lost my
8 You could
9 They had
10 They went

a) pictures of polar bears.
b) at five o'clock in the morning.
c) camp in the forest.
d) a map, but they got lost.
e) home two months after the start of the expedition.
f) of fish in the lake.
g) sailing in a small boat.
h) map, so I didn't know where to go.
i) a new island.
j) drink water from snow when you were thirsty.

2 Make a wordsearch puzzle.
Choose seven verbs.
Write them in the past
on the chart.
Write the verbs here:

find _____
can _____
_____
_____
_____
_____
_____

c											
o			f	o	u	n	d				
u											
l											
d											

3 Now look at your friend's wordsearch puzzle and find the words.

4 Ask and answer.

Could Vicky swim when she was three?

No, she couldn't.

Could Vicky swim when she was five?

Yes, she could.

5 Ask your friends and check (✓) or put an ✗.

Could you walk when you were one?

No, I couldn't.

Names	walk (1 year old)	talk (2 years old)	write (4 years old)	swim (5 years old)	read (6 years old)	ride a bike (8 years old)
Me						

6 Match and say.

1 He couldn't find his toothpaste,
2 She couldn't find her glasses,
3 He couldn't find his coat,
4 I couldn't find my camera,
5 We couldn't find our books,
6 She couldn't find her phone,

so

a we didn't do our homework.
b I couldn't take any pictures.
c she couldn't talk to her friend.
d he couldn't brush his teeth.
e she couldn't read her book.
f he had to wear a jacket.

7 Read and complete.

What's the opposite of ... ?

1 interesting
2 difficult
3 good
4 straight
5 clean
6 wrong
7 last
8 quiet
9 new

b	o	r	i	n	g

What's the secret word? _____

8 Read and match.

1 Danny's test is more difficult than Vicky's.
2 This movie is more exciting than that one.
3 The show about snails is more boring than the one about sharks.
4 She's more famous than he is.
5 She's more careful than he is.
6 Her homework is better than his.

9 Make sentences.

| thirsty | careful | happy | famous | ~~hungry~~ | strong | dirty |

1 Scott's hungrier than Sally.
2 --
3 --
4 --
5 --
6 --
7 --

10 Compare Tom's days. Choose words from the box.

| the weather (good / bad / sunny)   Tom (hungry / happy / tired) |
| the lesson (exciting / boring / difficult) |

Wednesday   Sunday

Tom was hungrier on
Wednesday than on Sunday.

11 **Write. Listen, check, and say.**

CD2

1 sh__ir__t	**2** p____son	**3** w____ld	**4** b____ger
5 n____se	**6** sk____t	**7** w____k	**8** l____n

12 **Match and color the squares.**

It's mine.

It's their garden.

gray

They're yours.

It's ours.

They're his trees.

pink

They're his.

They're hers.

It's my bike.

green

It's our world.

red

It's theirs.

They're your beaches.

purple

They're her plants.

blue

Ha! Ha! Ha!

Which side of a polar bear has more hair?

The outside.

JOKE BOX

Do you remember?

catch	_caught_	catch	→	caught
find	-----------	find	→	found
get	-----------	get	→	got
make	-----------	make	→	made
can	-----------	can	→	could
lose	-----------	lose	→	lost
come	-----------	come	→	came
careful	_more careful_	careful		more careful
difficult	-----------	difficult		more difficult
famous	-----------	famous		more famous
good	-----------	good		better
exciting	-----------	exciting		more exciting
boring	-----------	boring		more boring
easy	-----------	easy		easier

Can do

I can talk about events in the past.

I can compare people and things.

I can say what's mine and what's yours.

Science   Endangered animals

1 Read and match.

1 Polar bears are endangered because …

2 Brown bears are endangered because they're …

3 Some kinds of monkeys are endangered …

4 Whales are endangered …

5 Pandas are endangered because …

a … losing their habitat.

b … because oceans are getting dirtier.

c … it's difficult for them to get food.

d … oceans are getting hotter.

e … because forests are getting smaller.

2 Color the boxes and put the text in order.

pink	Arctic animals have a smaller habitat	yellow	
green	world changes the ice in the Arctic	brown	
red	bigger fish or sea animals to find	gray 1	
brown	and Antarctic to water. Polar bears and other	pink	
black	live in hotter water, so it's difficult for the	red	
orange 1	or walking. What other things can we do to help?	pink	
purple	hotter. Some small fish and sea animals can't	black	
gray 1	food. We can help by using bikes	orange 1	
orange 2	makes our world hotter. A hotter	green	
yellow	because the ice cap is smaller. The	gray 2	
white	Look at what happens when we use cars.	blue	1
gray 2	water in our oceans is also	purple	
blue	Cars make the air dirty and dirty air	orange 2	

Read the text. Choose the right words and write them on the lines.

Blue Whales

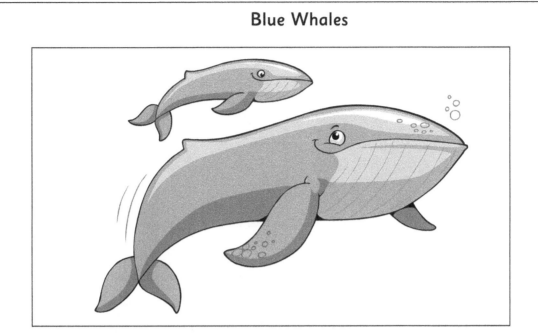

Example   Blue whales are blue or gray, and _____they_____ live in all the

1   oceans in the world. They _____ very small sea

           animals, small fish, and plants. Blue whales are bigger than

2   all other animals. _____ bodies are longer than

3   two buses, and they _____ very big mouths. About

           a hundred people can stand in a blue whale's mouth! On

4   _____ first day of its life, a baby blue whale is bigger

5   _____ a grown-up hippo. It drinks about four hundred

           liters of milk every day, and it grows very quickly.

Example   it   she   they
1   eat   eating   ate
2   Her   His   Their
3   had   have   having
4   the   a   some
5   then   that   than

6 Technology

1 Unscramble and write the words.

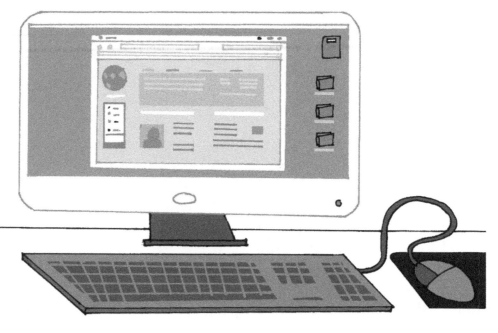

1 mcrtpoue	<u>computer</u>	**5** elima	_____
2 recens	_____	**6** rtneetlenht	_____
3 esumo	_____	**7** VDD	_____
4 utobnt	_____	**8** yrMa3Plpe	_____

2 Read and circle the correct answer.

KBX4 instructions

1 To turn on the computer you push the **mouse** / **screen** / (**button**).
2 Then you turn on the **screen** / **DVD** / **email**.
3 To find your place on the screen you move the **computer** / **MP3** / **mouse**.
4 You can write **an MP3 player** / **an email** / **a TV** to your friend.
5 You can look for information on the **mouse** / **Internet** / **button**.

3 **25** **Listen and write. There is one example.**
CD2

Shopping

1 Jack went shopping with his mom and _____

2 They bought _____

3 Who is it for? _____

4 He needs it to _____

5 It cost $ _____

4 **Write the sentences in order.**

1 ⟨ weren't ⟩⟨ years ago. ⟩⟨ any ⟩⟨ There ⟩⟨ one hundred ⟩⟨ cell phones ⟩

There weren't any cell phones one hundred years ago.

2 { you can } { use it. } { to turn on } { You have } { the computer } { before }

_____

3 { to text your friends } { It's easier } { emails. } { than write them }

_____

4 (can use) (to text) (You) (your) (a cell phone) (friends.)

_____

5 | listen to | | on our computers. | | We can | | music |

_____

6 { are } { than paper books. } { and smaller } { E-books } { better }

_____

7 (the Internet) (on) (use) (We can) (some cell phones.)

_____

5 Match. Write the words.

One of each is a past verb.

① bo**ught**

bo**ttle**

⑥ c_____

c_____

② ga_____

ga_____

⑦ d_____

d_____

③ w_____

w_____

⑧ p_____

p_____

④ ca_____

ca_____

⑨ kn_____

kn_____

⑤ th_____

th_____

⑩ ch_____

ch_____

~~ttle~~   reful

ough   rden

eather   inner

aught   icnic

~~ught~~

ent   id

ee

ut   ew

ve

ought   anks   ose

me   icken

6 Check six words. Play bingo.

BINGO!!! BINGO!!! BINGO!!! BINGO!!! BINGO!!! BINGO!!!

buy ☐	get ☐	have ☐	see ☐
catch ☐	bring ☐	is ☐	say ☐
choose ☐	go ☐	put ☐	take ☐
come ☐	know ☐	read ☐	think ☐

BINGO!!! BINGO!!! BINGO!!! BINGO!!! BINGO!!! BINGO!!!

6

7 **Answer the questions.**

1 Mary had forty-seven computer games. She gave her younger brother fifteen, and her older brother gave her twelve. How many does she have now?

forty-four

2 Farmer Green had eleven lemon trees and twenty orange trees. He bought eight more lemon trees on the Internet. How many trees did he have then? _____

3 Grandpa bought a new fishing DVD. Then he went fishing. He caught thirty-two fish, but he dropped eight in the river. How many fish did he take home? _____

4 Peter had twenty-five apps on his cell phone. He bought nineteen more apps on the Internet. He deleted four apps because he didn't like them. How many apps does he have now?

_____

8 **Match the questions and answers.**

1 What did they give their mother for her birthday?
2 Why did he put on his coat?
3 When did she take these pictures?
4 Which floor did they go up to?
5 Who did you see yesterday afternoon?
6 How many fish did Grandpa catch?
7 What time did you get up last Friday?

a They went up to the twelfth floor.
b We got up at eight o'clock.
c They gave her a red scarf.
d Because it was cold outside.
e He caught four.
f I saw my aunt.
g She took them last weekend.

9 Match the rhyming words. Listen, check, and say.

CD2

1	sport	_d_	**a)** water	6	door	_i_	**f)** talked
2	Paul	___	**b)** bought	7	smaller	___	**g)** fall
3	daughter	___	**c)** floor	8	walked	___	**h)** thought
4	caught	___	**d)** short	9	call	___	**i)** four
5	more	___	**e)** small	10	taught	___	**j)** taller

10 Make sentences.

~~We go~~	loves	cousin	was three.
I couldn't use	~~to the~~	computer for	on the Internet.
She	email their	when I	his mom.
He bought	a new	texting	in India.
They wanted to	a laptop	apps	~~every Saturday.~~
You chose	some	~~movies~~	her friends.

1   We go to the movies every Saturday.
2
3
4
5
6

 Ha! Ha! Ha!

Susan, your homework, "My computer," is the same as your brother's. Did you copy his?

No, sir, it's the same computer!

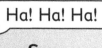 JOKE BOX

Do you remember?

 Look and read   Say   Fold the page    Write the words    Correct

bring   _brought_   bring → brought

buy   ------------------   buy → bought

choose   ------------------   choose → chose

read   ------------------   read → read

think   ------------------   think → thought

put   ------------------   put → put

say   ------------------   say → said

know   ------------------   know → knew

Can do

I can write "technology" words.

I can talk about computers and the Internet.

I can say more verbs in the past.

Technology Robots

1 Read and match. Write the sentences.

ⓐ

ⓑ

ⓒ

ⓓ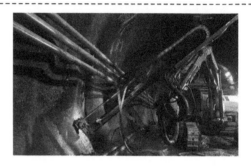

1 Robots can work underground.
2 Robots build things in factories.
3 Robots can help us explore space.
4 Robots can do jobs in the house for us.

2 Read and correct.

1 A robot is a machine that makes work more difficult for humans.
A robot is a machine that makes work easier for humans.

2 Robots can't do jobs that are dangerous.

---

3 Robots can't move around the house.

---

4 It's easier for robots to dance in factories.

---

5 Robots can't fix things.

---

6 Robots are always sick and tired.

---

3 Where did Charlie go with these people?
Listen and write a letter in each box. There is one example.

 Mom | H

 Aunt Daisy | ☐

 Dad | ☐

Lily | ☐

 Grandma | ☐

 Fred | ☐

 A

 B

 C

 D

 E

 F

 G

 H

Review Units 5 and 6

1 What can you see? Check the boxes.

moon ☐   orange ☐   river ☐   snail ☐   cage ☐   plant ☐

sweater ☐   blanket ☐   glass ☐   comic book ☐   road ☐

cup ✓

beard ☐   bottle ☐

CD ☐

dog ☐   sun ☐

picnic ☐   rock ☐

leaves ☐

parrot ☐   email ☐

banana ☐

mustache ☐

toothbrush ☐   rabbit ☐   grown-up ☐   uncle ☐

2 What can't you see? Write the words.

1 uncle _____   4 _____   7 _____
2 _____   5 _____   8 _____
3 _____   6 _____

3 Find the word. Use the first letters from Activity 2.

☐ ☐ ☐ ☐ u ☐ ☐ ☐

_____

4 Circle the one that doesn't belong.

1 bought	thought	brought	(sailed)
2 ticket	button	mouse	screen
3 plant	DVD	MP3	app
4 better	dirtier	quickly	funnier
5 bounced	between	behind	above
6 sharks	bears	whales	dolphins
7 river	cave	ocean	lake
8 drank	swam	liked	gave
9 Wednesday	evening	Sunday	Friday
10 was	were	went	where
11 weather	hotter	colder	quicker
12 came	made	found	know

5 Now complete the crossword puzzle. Write the message.

7 At the zoo

1 Make sentences.

The dolphin	lives	in	world.
Penguins	the loudest	ocean	the forest.
~~The polar bear~~	can't drink	animal in the	~~on the land~~.
The blue whale is	live	~~meat-eating animal~~	Antarctica.
The parrot	~~is the biggest~~	in	water.

1 *The polar bear is the biggest meat-eating animal on the land.*
2 _____
3 _____
4 _____
5 _____

2 Complete the text about the giraffe family.

father   mother   sister   brother   grandfather   aunt

In the giraffe family, _____Aunt_____ Giraffe is the most beautiful. _____ Giraffe is the tallest. _____ Giraffe is the youngest, and _____ Giraffe is the oldest . The smartest Giraffe in the family is _____ Giraffe. _____ Giraffe is the loudest giraffe in the family.

③ Which animal is it?

1 This is the tallest animal. It has four legs and a very long neck. _giraffe_____

2 It's the biggest land animal. It has two very big ears. -----------------

3 Some people think this is one of the most beautiful animals. It can fly. -----------------

4 This is the best animal at climbing trees. It can be very naughty, too. -----------------

5 This is the most dangerous animal. It can also swim. -----------------

6 This is the quickest animal here. It can also climb trees. -----------------

④ Ask questions and write the answers.

Ask four friends about their family.

	1	2	3	4
1 Who's the oldest?				
2 Who's the youngest?				
3 Who's the quietest?				
4 Who's the strongest?				
5 Who's the tallest?				
6 Who's the best at drawing?				
7 Who's the worst at singing?				
8 Who's the loudest?				

5 🔊37 CD2 **Listen and write the letter.**

① Kittens for Sale ② School ③ ④

⑤ School ⑥ ●000000000 ⑦ ⑧ ●000000000 a

6 **Make a wordsearch puzzle.**

Choose seven verbs. Write them in the past on the chart. Write the verbs here:

drive

fly

_____

_____

_____

_____

_____

d	r	o	v	e				
	f	l	e	w				

7 **Now look at your friend's wordsearch puzzle and find the words. Write three sentences with the words.**

1 _____

2 _____

3 _____

8 What did the animals do? Unscramble and write the words.

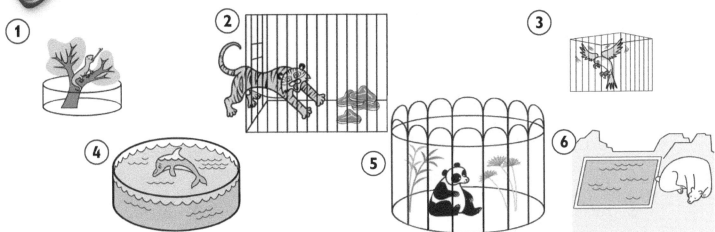

1 The lizard ~~tea~~ _ate_ the fly in the little round cage with a little tree in it.

2 The tiger *nar* _____ into the big square cage. There were a lot of big pieces of meat in it.

3 The parrot *lefw* _____ around the small square cage.

4 The dolphin *sawm* _____ quickly around the big round pool.

5 The panda *tsa* _____ in the big round cage. It was very clean.

6 The polar bear *epslt* _____ next to the big square pool.

9 Complete the sentences. Write "into," "out of," "along," or "around."

1 The train came _out of_ the station.

2 They flew _____ the bear's head.

3 Peter went _____ the library.

4 Mary came _____ the hospital.

5 The sharks swam _____ the island.

6 The cat walked _____ the wall.

10 📻 **Match the rhyming words. Listen, check, and say.**

CD2

1 school _d_	**a)** look	**6** whose _i_	**f)** blue
2 choose ____	**b)** two	**7** foot ____	**g)** book
3 zoo ____	**c)** could	**8** flew ____	**h)** balloon
4 took ____	**d)** pool	**9** moon ____	**i)** lose
5 good ____	**e)** shoes	**10** cook ____	**j)** put

 11 **Match the questions and answers.**

1 Did the kitten sleep in the yard yesterday?   **a** Yes, they do.
2 Could Stacey swim with the dolphins?   **b** Yes, they can.
3 Was there a shark at the zoo?   **c** No, it didn't.
4 Do monkeys climb better than bears?   **d** Yes, they could.
5 Can bears swim?   **e** No, there wasn't.
6 Were the elephants the biggest animals at the zoo?   **f** Yes, they were.
7 Did Zoe's dad walk along the beach yesterday?   **g** No, she couldn't.
8 Could the children feed the parrots at the zoo?   **h** Yes, he did.

12 **Ask and answer.**

What's the past of drive?

Drove.

What's the past of … ?

Ha! Ha! Ha!

JOKE BOX

What time is it when an elephant sits on your bed?

Time to get a new bed!

Do you remember?

_in_ _____	in
_____	above
_____	below
_____	in front of
_____	behind
_____	next to
_____	between
_____	across from
_____	along
_____	out of
_____	around

Can do

I can say more verbs in the past.

I can talk about animals at the zoo.

I can talk about the biggest, the best, and the tallest things.

1 Match. Write the word.

dog horse bat bear whale rabbit

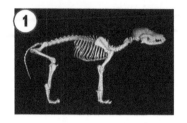

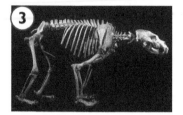

dog

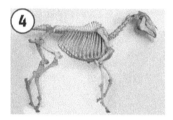

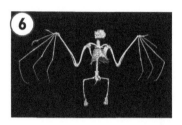

2 Write the sentences in order.

1 has the | A giraffe | of neck | same number | bones as a human.

A giraffe has the same number of neck bones as a human.

2 have | and legs. | Some monkeys | long arms

3 swim. | A crocodile's | helps it | strong | tail

4 is all an | together. | animal's bones | A skeleton

5 Crocodiles | eyes on the top | of their heads. | have big

6 the human | bone in | skeleton is | The longest | in the leg.

3 Read the text and choose the best answer.
Sally is talking to her friend Jack.

Example
Sally: What are you reading, Jack?
Jack: A No, I'm not.
        B A book about animals.
        C I'm writing.

Questions
1 Sally: Do you like animals?
   Jack: A I don't have a dog.
            B No, thanks.
            C I love them.

2 Sally: Which is your favorite animal?
   Jack: A Whales are the ugliest.
            B I really love tigers.
            C I don't like chocolate.

3 Sally: Why do you like them?
   Jack: A I think they're the most beautiful animals.
            B I don't think so.
            C I'd like some fries, please.

4 Sally: Did you go to the zoo last week?
   Jack: A Yes, we went on Friday afternoon.
            B Yes, we do.
            C Yes, every Saturday.

5 Sally: What did you do there?
   Jack: A We see the elephants.
            B We don't see the lions.
            C We saw the kangaroos.

6 Sally: Hmm. Do you want **an apple**?
   Jack: A Yes, please. I like **apples**.
            B OK. What color?
            C Yes, a banana.

8 Let's party!

1 Circle the one that doesn't belong.

1 a cup of:	tea	(bananas)	coffee	milk
2 a bag of:	fruit	candy	potatoes	water
3 a bowl of:	soup	salad	noodles	orange juice
4 a glass of:	lemonade	milk	milkshake	apples
5 a bottle of:	water	pears	sauce	lemonade
6 a box of:	cupcakes	chocolates	eggs	chicken

2 Unscramble and write the words.

1 There's a ~~rcntoa of sgeg~~. *carton of eggs* _____

2 There's a *pcu* of *efcoef*. _____

3 There's a *lsags* of *limk*. _____

4 There's a *gba* of *spare*. _____

5 There's a *tetlob* of *ratwe*. _____

6 There's a *lwbo* of *iturf*. _____

7 There's a *xbo* of *aresong*. _____

72

3 Write sentences.

1 <u>Scott wants Sally to open the window.</u>
2
3
4
5
6

 **4** Listen, color, and write. There is one example.

5 Choose your party.

Last week was | Jack's / Ann's / Paul and Mary's | ninth / tenth / eleventh | birthday. I went

to | his / her / their | party last | Saturday / Wednesday / Friday | . It was | good / exciting / nice | . We ate

| pasta / sandwiches / pancakes | and drank | fruit juice / lemonade / water | . We | played / saw / sang | a funny | song / movie / game | .

I gave | him / her / them | a book / a CD / a soccer ball | . I came home at | seven / eight / nine | o'clock.

6 Look at the picture. Write "yes" or "no."

1 The man with the mustache is talking the most quietly.   _yes_____

2 The younger girl is riding the most carefully.   _____

3 The woman wearing glasses is shouting the most loudly.   _____

4 The boys are riding the best.   _____

5 The older girl is riding the most quickly.   _____

6 The man with the beard is riding the most slowly.   _____

7 **Read and complete the chart.**

Vicky had a party yesterday. All the children wore costumes. After the party, Vicky's mom couldn't find the children. Can you help her?

1 The girl who didn't wear pants wore a little white hat.
2 The girl who had a black beard wore white pants.
3 A boy had a big red nose.
4 A girl wore a big black hat.
5 The boy who wore red pants also wore an orange hat.
6 Vicky wore a white dress.

Name	pants	dress	hat	nose	beard
Susan					
Peter					
Vicky			little white		

Who was the clown? ---------------------------------
Who was the pirate? ---------------------------------
Who was the nurse? ---------------------------------

8 **Find three words from the same group.** ↓ → ↘ ↗

①
~~panda~~	~~lion~~	~~giraffe~~
doctor	worst	bought
movie star	drove	nurse

②
model	jumped	longest
kicked	tallest	pirate
best	whale	shark

③
dentist	ate	panda
better	drank	fish
monkey	went	clown

④
pirate	had	snake
could	clown	was
bat	parrot	pop star

9 **Write. Listen, check, and say.**

CD3

| eggs | vegetables | sandwich | wanted | terrible | good | computer |
| quickly | flew | basketball | easy | caught | enjoy | came | difficult |

one syllable	two syllables	three syllables
eggs	sandwich	vegetables

  10 **Listen and check the box.**

CD3

1 (a)  (b)  ✓ (c)

2 (a)  (b)  (c)

3 (a)  (b)  (c)

4 (a)  (b)  (c)

Ha! Ha! Ha!

JOKE BOX

Which are the strongest days of the week?

Saturday and Sunday, because the others are weekdays.

76

Do you remember?

 tea   tea

 _____   milkshake

 _____   pancakes

 _____   vegetables

 _____   cheese

 _____   salad

_____   sauce

 _____   noodles

 _____   glass

_____   cup

_____   bottle

_____   bowl

 _____   box

Can do

I can say more food and container words.

I can talk about things I want someone to do.

I can talk about parties.

1 Put the words in groups.

chicken rice noodles milk grapes fish bananas apples eggs
beans peas cake chocolate carrots yogurt bread candy

carbohydrates	protein	fruit and vegetables	dairy products	fats and sugars
	chicken			

2 Read and write.

1 Susan's having a baby. She needs a lot of protein. What kinds of food does she have to eat?
   She has to eat fish, chicken, beans, and eggs.

2 Tom's always hungry. He eats chocolate between meals. What different kinds of food can he eat?
   _____

3 Danny runs every day. He needs a lot of energy. What must he eat?
   _____

4 Vicky has a cold. She needs some vitamins to make her better. What must she eat?
   _____

5 Ben has a problem with his teeth. He needs to make them stronger. What must he eat?
   _____

3 🎧 **15** **CD3** Listen and draw lines. There is one example.

Danny   May   Jack   Kim

Bill   Jane   Paul

Review Units 7 and 8

1 Find the past of the verbs.

~~are~~   find   ride

buy   fly   run

catch   get   say

choose   give   see

come   go   sing

do   have   sit

draw   is   sleep

drink   know   swim

drive   put   take

eat   read   think

w	d	o	f	a	s	r	a	t	o	o	k
a	i	d	l	g	a	v	e	h	i	n	o
s	d	r	e	w	i	d	t	o	m	s	o
b	f	a	w	e	d	r	p	u	a	a	c
g	e	n	i	n	b	o	u	g	h	t	f
c	a	k	e	t	o	v	t	h	a	m	o
a	t	e	r	s	l	e	p	t	d	o	u
u	k	n	e	w	a	t	s	r	a	n	n
g	o	t	s	a	l	c	h	o	s	e	d
h	n	c	a	m	e	a	t	d	a	t	i
t	o	o	w	r	e	a	d	t	n	n	t
w	e	r	e	h	r	o	d	e	g	a	c

2 Read and choose the picture.

Frank can't find his bag. Can you help him? His bag has two books and a box of pencils in it. He has two small bottles of water, an orange, and his favorite comic book. Which one is his?

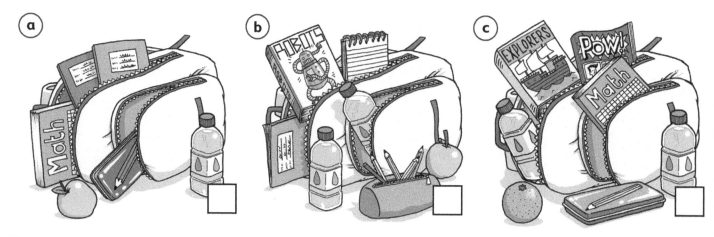

a   b   c

3 Now describe to your friend what's in one of the other bags.

4 Circle one that doesn't belong.

1 tired	thirsty	awake	(badly)
2 carry	climbed	copy	cry
3 twelve	third	eighth	twentieth
4 quickly	well	Friday	slowly
5 tea	coffee	juice	vegetable
6 fries	bottle	cup	glass
7 DVD	movie	DVD player	sweater
8 when	who	were	why
9 soup	ate	pasta	sandwich
10 swam	flew	sat	through
11 dolphin	beard	bat	parrot

5 Now complete the crossword puzzle. Write the message.

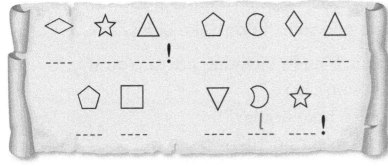

1 🔊 17 CD3 Listen and number.

2 Read and choose.

1 When people help you, …

   a) you look at your watch and say, "Is that the time?"

   b) you smile and say, "Thank you."

   c) you say, "Can I have an apple, please?"

2 After your birthday party, …

   a) you say thank you to your parents and help to clean the living room.

   b) you sit on the couch and watch TV.

   c) you have another piece of cake and play with your new toys.

3 In a café, the man gives you your lunch and says, "Enjoy your food."

   a) You look at your lunch and start to eat.

   b) You smile and say, "Thank you."

   c) You look at your parents and say, "I don't like cafés."

4 You're going home after your friend's birthday party. You say,

   a) "Where's my coat? My mom's here."

   b) "Can I have that balloon to take home?"

   c) "Thanks a lot. That was a great party."

Read and complete.

| Would you like to sit down? | Can you help me, please? |
| Should I carry your shopping? | What's the matter? |

a

b

c

d

② **Read and choose.**

1 When Jack sees an old person standing on the bus, he always **sits down** / (**stands up**) for them.

2 When Stacey sees a younger child with a problem, she always **helps** / **takes** a picture.

3 When Jim goes to the supermarket with his grandpa, he always **opens** / **carries** the shopping bags.

4 When Vicky plays at the park, she always **shares** / **breaks** things with the other children.

5 When someone helps Daisy, she always says **"Thank you."** / **"Goodbye."**

1 Look and write. What dangerous things can you see?

1 <u>The woman is listening to music and running into the road.</u>

2 ....

3 ....

4 ....

5 ....

2 Put the words in order.

1 | It's dangerous | the road. | to roller-skate on |

<u>It's dangerous to roller-skate on the road.</u>

2 | cross the | You must not | cars. | road between |

....

3 | the road at | must cross | You | a crosswalk. |

....

4 | close to busy | You must not | roads. | play |

....

5 | your bike. | Wear bright | helmet on | colors and a |

....

1 Read and match.

1 We can make new things from old things.

2 Always put glass bottles in a recycling bin.

3 People make bottles, bowls, and glasses from recycled glass.

4 Don't put the wrong things in the recycling bins.

5 Make plastic bottles smaller before you recycle them.

6 When you can't reuse old clothes, you can recycle them.

2 Look and write. What good things are the people doing?

1 The girl is reusing the clothes.

2 _____

3 _____

4 _____

Grammar reference

⭐ Read and complete.

1 I think badminton is _ _ _ _ _ _ _ _ _ _ than tennis. (easy)
2 My aunt is _ _ _ _ _ _ _ _ _ _ than my dad. (young)
3 The black cat is _ _ _ _ _ _ _ _ _ _ than the white one. (thin)
4 Scott's hair is _ _ _ _ _ _ _ _ _ _ than Sally's hair. (short)

1 Look and complete. (singing   are   who   's)

1 He's the boy who _ _ _ _ _ _ _ _ _ _ reading.
2 They're the girls who _ _ _ _ _ _ _ _ _ _ playing.
3 This is the man _ _ _ _ _ _ _ _ _ _ works at the hospital.
4 She's the woman who's _ _ _ _ _ _ _ _ _ _ .

2 Read and order the words. Make sentences.

(dance.) (can) (You) (learn) (to)

1 _

(to) (He) (learn) (to swim.) (wants)

2 _

(to) (It's) (can) (a place) (learn) (you) (sail.) (where)

3 _

(want) (They) (don't) (ice-skating.) (to learn)

4 _

3 Look and complete. (did   ate   eat   didn't   Yes)

Mom: Did you _ _ _ _ _ _ _ _ _ _ the cookies?
Tom: _ _ _ _ _ _ _ _ _ _ , I did.
Mom: How many _ _ _ _ _ _ _ _ _ _ you have?
Tom: I _ _ _ _ _ _ _ _ _ _ four cookies.
Mom: Did Dad drink the juice?
Tom: No, he _ _ _ _ _ _ _ _ _ _ . I drank the juice, too!

86

4 Read and circle the correct answer.

1 Grandma **danced** / **dancing** yesterday!
2 I **tried** / **trying** to sing the song.
3 She **drop** / **dropped** her books on the floor.
4 We watched the movie and **laughs** / **laughed**.

5 Read and circle the correct answer.

1 I read more **slow** / **slowly** than my brother.
2 He writes more **carefully** / **careful** than she does.
3 We are **good** / **better** than they are at soccer.
4 The teacher speaks more **loud** / **loudly** than the students.

6 Read and complete.

Today was my birthday, and my parents (1) _ _ _ _ _ _ _ _ _ _ _ (buy) me an
MP3 player. I (2) _ _ _ _ _ _ _ _ _ _ _ (put) it in my bag and (3) _ _ _ _ _ _ _ _ _ _ _
(catch) the bus to school. When I (4) _ _ _ _ _ _ _ _ _ _ _ (go) into the
classroom, I wanted to show it to my friends, but it wasn't in my bag!
The teacher (5) _ _ _ _ _ _ _ _ _ _ _ (say), "Let's help!" Everyone looked for my
present, but we couldn't find it. At lunchtime my brother (6) _ _ _ _ _ _ _ _ _ _ _
(bring) me my MP3 player. I didn't put it in my bag, I put it in his!

7 Match the sentences.

1 Where did you eat lunch?   a) I drew three pictures.
2 Who did they see?   b) I ate it at school.
3 What did you draw?   c) They saw their uncle.

8 Look and complete.

the best   most loudly   worst   most carefully

1 Ben writes the _ _ _ _ _ _ _ _ _ _ _ _ _ _ _ _ _ in our class.
2 My drawing is the _ _ _ _ _ _ _ _ _ _ _ _ _ _ _ _ _ . It's terrible!
3 You play your MP3 player the _ _ _ _ _ _ _ _ _ _ _ _ _ _ _ _ _ .
4 She plays badminton _ _ _ _ _ _ _ _ _ _ _ _ _ _ _ _ .

Irregular verbs

Infinitive	Past tense	Infinitive	Past tense
be	was/were	know	knew
be called	was/were called	lose	lost
bring	brought	make	made
buy	bought	mean	meant
can	could	must	had to
catch	caught	put	put
choose	chose	put on	put on
come	came	read	read
do	did	ride	rode
draw	drew	run	ran
drink	drank	say	said
drive	drove	see	saw
dry	dried	sing	sang
eat	ate	sit	sat
fall	fell	sleep	slept
find	found	stand	stood
fly	flew	swim	swam
get	got	take	took
get (un)dressed	got (un)dressed	take a picture	took a picture
get (up/on/off)	got (up/on/off)	take off	took off
give	gave	tell	told
go	went	think	thought
go shopping	went shopping	throw	threw
have	had	understand	understood
have to	had to	wake up	woke up
hide	hid	wear	wore
hit	hit	write	wrote
hold	held		
hurt	hurt		

About me

My birthday: --

Where I live: ---

Languages I know

Interesting!

Great!

Write the languages you know.
Check (✓) the boxes.

Language: -------------------------------------

I speak this language:

at home ☐   at school ☐   on the street ☐   on vacations ☐

Language: -------------------------------------

I speak this language:

at home ☐   at school ☐   on the street ☐   on vacations ☐

Language: -------------------------------------

I speak this language:

at home ☐   at school ☐   on the street ☐   on vacations ☐

Other languages: --

My English language skills

1 What do you do in English? Complete the sentences.

Listening	I listen to _English songs_ . I listen to _____ .	☺
Reading	I read _____ _____ .	☺
Speaking	I speak to _____ _____ .	☺
Writing	I write _____ _____ .	☺

2 Do you like doing these things in English? Color the faces.

Yellow = It's fantastic.   Green = It's OK.

Blue = It's good.   Red = It's difficult.

I can ...   Units 1-2

1  Listen and number.

2 Say. Tell your friend about someone in the class. Don't say their name. Can they guess who it is?

> This person is tall. She has long black hair ...

3 Read and match. Write the numbers.

1 Yes, I do.   2 No, I don't.   3 Yes, I can.

a Can you play the guitar?   3

b Do you live in New York?

c Do you have a lot of brothers and sisters?

d Do you like spiders?

e Do you have a pet?

f Can you play tennis?

4 Write about you.

What do you look like? What do you have?
What do you like? What can you do?

Check (✓): I can do it!	
Easily	With help
1	
2	
3	
4	

I can ...   # Units 3–4

Check (✓): I can do it!		
	Easily	With help
1		
2		
3		
4		

1 Listen and say.

 a 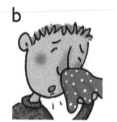 b  c  d

2 Ask your friend the questions.

(Did you play a game yesterday?)

1 play / game / yesterday?
2 eat / fruit and vegetables / yesterday?
3 what / do / after dinner / last night?

3 Read about the school club. Answer the questions.

Come to the school photography club!

Do you have a camera? Do you like taking pictures?
Then this is the club for you. Pay $2.00.
Bring your camera. We meet every Friday after school
in the library, from 4:30 to 6:30.

a Where does the club meet? _____
b When does it meet? _____
c What do you have to bring? _____
d How much does it cost? _____

4 Write about your club.

My club is _____
_____

I can ...

Units 5–6

Check (✓): I can do it!	
Easily	With help
1	
2	
3	
4	

1  Listen and check (✓). What did Sam do?

a  ☐   b ☐   c  ☐

d ☐   e ☐   f  ☐

2 💬 Say. Compare two things.

> The movie theater is better than watching TV because ...

movie theater	TV
mountains	beach
a pet snake	a pet dog
traveling by plane	traveling by bus

3 🔍 Read and complete.

brush   train   ~~world~~   paper   walk   off

Help protect the 1 _world_ . Turn off the faucet when you
2 _____ your teeth. Catch a bus or a 3 _____ .
Go to school on your bike. Or you can 4 _____ ! Turn
5 _____ the lights when you go out of a room. Put your
glass, 6 _____ , and cans in special recycling bins.

4 ✏️ Write about your last English class.
What activities did you do? What did you learn?

_____

_____

I can ...   # Units 7–8

1  Listen to the descriptions and say the names.

Jack

Laura

Kate

2 Say. Tell your partner what you did yesterday. Use the words in the speech bubbles.

> In the morning I ...
> In school ... I ate ...
> I didn't ...

> In the afternoon I ...
> I played ... I walked ...
> I didn't ...

3 Read the recipe for a ham and cheese sandwich. Order the sentences.

- [ ] Cut the sandwich in half and eat it. Yum!
- [ ] Cut the ham and cheese.
- [ ] Put the top on the sandwich.
- [1] Put butter on the bread.
- [ ] Put the ham and cheese on the bread.

4 Write a party invitation.

> **✿✿✿✿ Come to my party! ✿✿✿✿**
>
> When _____
> Where _____
> Why _____
> Food and drink _____
> _____

Check (✓): I can do it!	
Easily	With help
1	
2	
3	
4	

Learning English

What do you like doing in English classes? Write "yes," "no," or "sometimes" under the pictures.

Working in pairs and groups

Working alone

Using the book

Taking tests

Listening to the teacher

Listening to CDs

Practicing pronunciation

Reading books

Doing projects

Doing arts and crafts

Acting

Speaking in groups and pairs

Singing songs

Playing games

Watching DVDs

My interests

Draw or stick a picture of something you like doing.

What hobby, sport, or interest did you choose? _____

Where do you do it? _____

Why do you like it? _____

Who do you do it with? _____

_____

What do you need in order to do it? _____

_____

Our club

Draw a picture of your club.

What's your club called? _____

Where do you meet? _____

What time do you meet? _____

What do you need to bring? _____

_____

What do you do there? _____

A short story

Write and draw a story. It can be about something that happened to you, or you can use your imagination.

You need an introduction (1), a middle (2 and 3), and an ending (4).

Title: _____

By: _____

1 _____ _____ _____	2 _____ _____ _____
3 _____ _____ _____	4 _____ _____ _____

What's the best invention?

Draw or stick a picture of your favorite invention.

I like this invention because --

It's better than -- because ------------------------

With this invention you can --- ,

but you can't --

I have this invention: yes / no.

99

A place I like

Draw or stick a picture of your favorite place.

Is it inside or outside? Is it a room in your home? Is it the movie theater or a park? Is it the beach or the mountains?

Where is it? _____

When did you last go there? _____

What did you do there the last time you went? _____

_____

_____

_____

A special event

Write about something special you did.

Was it a celebration (a street party, a birthday party, or a wedding)?

Was it a day out (a picnic, a walk in the country, a shopping trip, or a day at the zoo)?

Did you go out at night (to a concert, the movies, or the theater)?

What was your special event? _____

Who went with you? _____

When did you go? _____

What did you do? _____

_____

Thanks and Acknowledgments

Authors' thanks

Many thanks to everyone at Cambridge University Press and in particular to:

Rosemary Bradley, for overseeing the whole project and succesfully pulling it all together with good humor.

Camilla Agnew, for her fine editorial skills and tireless dedication to the project.

Jason Mann, for his valuable input and support.

Karen Elliott, for her enthusiasm and creative reworking of the Phonics sections.

A special thanks to all our students at Star English, El Palmar, Murcia, and especially to our colleague, Jim Kelly, for his help, suggestions, and support at various stages of the project.

Dedications

For Teresa and Giuseppe Vincenti for all their wholehearted support and encouragement, with much love and thanks – CN

To Javi, Maria José, and Laura. Thanks for all the appreciation, enthusiasm, and avid interest along the way, but above all for your friendship – MT

The authors and publishers would like to thank the following teachers for their help in reviewing the material and for the invaluable feedback they provided:

Claudio Almada, Argentina; Sandra Carvalho Araujo, Brazil; Marcelo D'Elia, Brazil; Gustavo Antonio Castro Arenal, Mexico; Rocio Licea Ayala, Mexico; Gilda Castro, Spain; Ana BeatrizIzquierdo Hurbado, Spain; Ruth Mura, Turkey.

The authors and publishers would like to thank the following consultants for their invaluable feedback:

Pippa Mayfield, Hilary Ratcliff, Melanie Williams.

We would also like to thank all the teachers who allowed us to observe their classes and who gave up their invaluable time for interviews and focus groups.

The authors and publishers acknowledge the following sources of copyright material and are grateful for the permissions granted. While every effort has been made, it has not always been possible to identify the sources of all the material used, or to trace all copyright holders.
If any omissions are brought to our notice, we will be happy to include the appropriate acknowledgments on reprinting.

p. 34 (1 a): Shutterstock/© sheff; p. 34 (2 a): Alamy/© Jack Cox in Spain; p. 34 (2 b): Shutterstock/© Jason Stitt; p. 34 (2 c): Alamy/© CenLu; p. 34 (3 b): Shutterstock/© Piotr Marcinski; p. 34 (4 c): Shutterstock/© Jason Stitt; p. 60 (a): Shutterstock/© John Kasawa; p. 60 (b): Alamy/© B.A.E Inc; p. 60 (c): Alamy/© Jim West; p. 60 (d): Getty Images/© E+/Eduard Andras; p. 70 (1): Shutterstock/© sippakorn; p. 70 (2): Shutterstock/© Philip Lange; p. 70 (3): SuperStock/© Biosphoto; p. 70 (4): Getty Images/© Dorling Kindersley/Dave King; p. 70 (5): Alamy/© Urban Zone; p. 70 (6): Shutterstock/© Waddell Images

Commissioned photography on pages 20, 34 (1 b), 34 (1 c), 34 (3 a), 34 (3 c), 34 (4 a), 34 (4 b), 68 by Trevor Clifford photography.

The authors and publishers are grateful to the following illustrators:

Adrian Barclay, c/o Beehive; Andrew Painter; Alan Rowe; Anthony Rule; Bryan Beach, c/o Advocate Art; James Walmesley, c/o Graham-Cameron Illustration; Gwyneth Williamson; Trevor Metcalfe; Julian Mosedale, Ken Oliver c/o Art Agency; Melanie Sharp, c/o Syvlie Poggio; Nigel Dobbyn, c/o Beehive; R&C Burrows, c/o Beehive; Christos Skaltsas (hyphen); Lisa Smith, c/o Sylvie Poggio; F&L Productions

The publishers are grateful to the following contributors:

Louise Edgeworth: picture research and art direction
Wild Apple Design Ltd: page design
Blooberry: additional design
Lon Chan: cover design
Melanie Sharp: cover illustration
John Green and Tim Woolf, TEFL Audio: audio recordings
Songs written and produced by Robert Lee, Dib Dib Dub Studios. John Marshall Media, Inc. and Lisa Hutchins: audio recordings for the American English edition
hyphen S.A.: publishing management, American English edition